DADI JANKI

COMPANION
OF GOD

ABOUT THE AUTHOR

DADI JANKI is the Administrative Head of the Brahma Kumaris World Spiritual University (BKWSU) and a world-renowned spiritual leader. She travels worldwide, teaching and sharing her wisdom and deep knowledge of the science of spirituality. Driven by her vision of a better world, Dadi Janki has dedicated the past 73 years of her life to uplifting humanity. She campaigns for truth and works tirelessly for world peace. Dadi is one of the 'Keepers of Wisdom', an eminent group of spiritual and religious leaders convened to advise political leaders on spiritual dilemmas underpinning current worldwide issues of the environment and human settlement.

Dadi Janki is a visionary whose uniqueness lies in her unswerving optimism and a heart that is rich with compassion. Through understanding spiritual truths, she has come to a position of personal peace and power. She is a soul who refuses to set limits and boundaries as to what is achievable and, in so doing, inspires others to believe that they too can make the impossible, possible.

Dadi has pioneered the development of several international projects (in 129 countries) developing vision, values and action at a grass roots level, empowering individuals and communities to improve their own quality of life and the environment.

Now 94 years of age, Dadi Janki is still spiritually vivacious. Her diary is usually packed with international itineraries, which take her from Asia to South America and Europe to South Africa. Even when she has a few days to spare, whether at her base in London or the Headquarters in Mount Abu, India, she makes sure they are filled with some form of spiritual service. Her generosity and tirelessness are an inspiration to all.

ABOUT BRAHMA KUMARIS
WORLD SPIRITUAL UNIVERSITY

THE BRAHMA KUMARIS World Spiritual University is an international organisation working at all levels of society for positive change. Established in 1937, the University now has more than 8,500 centres in more than 100 countries.

Acknowledging the intrinsic worth and goodness of the inner self, the University teaches a practical method of meditation that helps people to cultivate their inner strengths and values. The University has local centres around the world offering courses and seminars that encourage spirituality in daily life and cover topics such as positive thinking, anger management, stress relief and self esteem. This spiritual approach is also brought into healthcare, social work, education, prisons and other community settings.

The University's Academy in Mount Abu, Rajasthan, India, offers individuals from all backgrounds a variety of life-long learning opportunities to help them recognise their inherent qualities and abilities in order to make the most of their lives. The University also supports the Global Hospital and Research Centre in Mount Abu.

All courses and activities are offered free of charge.

www.bkwsu.org
www.bkwsu.org.uk

DADI JANKI

COMPANION
OF GOD

Designed by Sameer Patro
Illustrations by Alice Evans
Printed by Srinivas Fine Arts (P) Ltd., Sivakasi, India

TO BAPDADA

We thank you for this original and beautifully polished 'jewel'
and all the jewels of wisdom she has given to all of us.

CONTENTS

DADI JANKI

A SPIRITUAL LEADER

DADI JANKI is a woman of wisdom... A woman who, through the understanding of spiritual truths, has reached a position of personal peace and power. In a world which is teetering on the edge of extreme chaos, Dadi Janki has discovered her own personal world of balance and order.

Now in her nineties, Dadi Janki is internationally acknowledged as a great spiritual leader, teacher and mentor who continues to offer inspiration to many people searching for peace and harmony in their heart and homeland.

As Administrative Head of the Brahma Kumaris World Spiritual University (BKWSU), Dadi Janki provides a working leadership model for all women and men who are seeking to integrate both male and female qualities into their personal and professional lives. Dadi lovingly engages people of all faiths and walks of life to be true to their spiritual self; to undertake their unique and individual part in the play of creating the future – a world worthy of the generations to come. In short, Dadi Janki calls us all to our potential.

'What kind of world is forming now, beyond this winter of war and sorrow, of poverty, pollution and death? In the winter, we foresee the spring. Those with a positive vision of the future give us an image of a world on this planet where all things are given freely, where the highest human potential is fully realised. But we can get to that stage only when there are leaders to take us there.'

DADI JANKI

International acknowledgment of Dadi's work came in 1992 when she was invited to be one of the 10 Keepers of Wisdom, an eminent group of world spiritual leaders convened to advice the Earth Summit in Brazil on the fundamental spiritual dilemmas which underpin current worldwide environmental issues.

Dadi Janki has dedicated her life to the service of humanity. She began her spiritual apprenticeship in 1937 at the age of 21 and was one of the founding members of the BKWSU. She spent 14 years in an enclosed community where intense meditation practice and the study of spiritual knowledge provided her with a firm foundation for the future. Dadi's purest wish is that all people find the inherent truth of their own spirituality and, as such, realise the potential of their personal relationship with God, the Supreme Soul. In essence, this is the foundation of her lifelong work.

Through the BKWSU, which Dadi administers, the ancient Eastern principles of Raja Yoga are taught. The fulcrum of Raja Yoga is a silent form of meditation which over the past 41 years has provided many interested people outside India with an opportunity to understand and appreciate more deeply their values, their vision for themselves, their future and their faith. Dadi Janki has been an instrumental in bringing and translating this valuable self-management philosophy from the mystic realm of India to the hard-nosed, practical arena of our modern world.

Most of all, Dadi Janki is a visionary whose uniqueness lies in her unswerving optimism and a heart rich in compassion. She is a soul who refuses to set limits and boundaries as to what is achievable and in so doing inspires others to believe that they too can make the impossible possible.

THE SOURCE OF WISDOM

If one were to ask Dadi Janki the question, 'How did you acquire such a wisdom and was it personal research, divine intuition or lessons learnt from life?' Dadi's answer would probably be to point her finger up above to indicate that the knowledge she shares has come from one Source. On further questioning, she would reveal that gurus, scriptures and devotion have not provided her with answers to the questions in her mind, but that her understanding has come from the knowledge revealed by the Supreme through the physical instrument of Prajapita Brahma, the founder of the BKWSU.

Dadi remembers her experience of deep love for God from the age of 2 years. Her search for Truth began at the age of 11, and continued until she saw Brahma Baba after his own dramatic transformation. As a girl, she had known Brahma Baba since he studied and discussed the esoteric secrets of the scriptures with her uncles and relatives. At the age of 19, walking in a park, she met Baba again. An intense bright light emanated from this person and Dadi was transfixed and knew instinctively that something divine and magical had transformed this man. From that moment, Brahma Baba became the instrument to share God's Truth, in words, vibrations and actions.

Over the years, Dadi's own relationship with God has deepened to the point of constant awareness through the inspiration and guidance of Brahma Baba. Often in challenging situations, Dadi would ask herself – 'How would Baba deal with this?' – and the image and activity of Brahma Baba would help her resolve the problem.

Today, Dadi is motivated by the desire to bring souls to God and share the enthusiasm and energy which she gives this task, as coming from the example of Brahma Baba. It was Brahma Baba's total surrender and obedience to God, his humility, generosity of spirit and purity of heart which are the guiding principles for Dadi and the students of BKWSU even now.

A WOMAN OF WISDOM AND
A TEACHER OF TEACHERS

A personal account of Dadi Janki by Sister Jayanti

IS IT POSSIBLE for a mortal to make God their constant friend? Dadi Janki has demonstrated that it is possible to have such a living relationship filled with spirituality. This perhaps has been Dadi's greatest contribution to the lives of thousands of people – to transform the image of God from a distant figure of fear and awe to a loving Parent and wise Teacher who cares, supports, nurtures and uplifts each one. She can be described perhaps as an electrician – one who can repair the broken links, reconnect the wires of the soul with the Supreme Source of Light and Might, the Powerhouse who is God.

With humility and a heart so clear that it sees only the goodness of each human being; Dadi has absorbed Truth from God so deeply that each breath and each moment is filled with that wisdom. Destiny brought me into contact with Dadi at the age of 8. As a child, the predominant memories are of Dadi's love and generous heart – constantly sharing physical and spiritual gifts. Dadi's stability and consistent yogi life were a reference point during my adolescent years of turbulent change. At the time when I was ready to listen, Dadi shared insights that opened up the closed doors of perception.

Events brought Dadi and myself to London together in April 1974. Living with Dadi day and night has been an incredible fortune that empowered the soul to learn, stretch, grow and evolve. I have observed Dadi playing with the jewels of spiritual knowledge and sharing them at each moment. Dadi is never too tired or too busy; it's never too late. She keeps her personal channel always clear and open, so that God's light and love constantly fills her. She then manages to step out of the way, so that this light and love flow across to each one who enters her sphere of contact. Being a translator for Dadi for several years has been a unique education and training. I would be a 'fly on the wall' – observing souls come in confusion and distress and leave with clarity, joy and strength. Each day Dadi would deal with hundreds, sometimes thousands of people and she would listen to each with great regard and respect, ultimately enabling them to see facets of themselves that they had not been able to see alone. Sometimes her patience would be challenged, sometimes her trust, but Dadi has never yet lost hope for souls or let go of her trust in them. She recognises their qualities more clearly than they themselves do and enables them to fulfil their potential. It was with good reason that the founder of this institution, Brahma Baba, entrusted her with the role of being the teacher of teachers.

Dadi's power of communication extends far beyond the words she uses. It is a fact that each word spoken comes from the depth of her experience and application. However, it is her experiment with the power of silence that has the greatest impact. Her power of silence filled with God's love and joy has visibly changed the attitudes of people. The depth of stillness emanating from her presence has answered many questions. Her power of silence has made vision and dreams a practical reality, dissolving many obstacles that come in the way.

Dadi Janki demonstrates the method of transcending all limits – age, health, gender, personality and nature – of living under the canopy of God's love and sharing that protection with all.

Sister Jayanti
European Director, Brahma Kumaris

PART 1

FIRST STEPS ON
THE SPIRITUAL PATH

DADI'S FIRST THOUGHTS...

THE FOUNDATION of our relationship should be one of friendship. When architects build buildings, they plan for them to last for a long time and so take care of all the small details; they don't do the work just for the sake of doing it. In the same way, the quality of our interactions should be such that our friendships and relationships last a long time; this requires us to have good wishes and pure feelings for everyone from the start and to see their goodness. When we have such good wishes and pure feelings towards others, then whatever weaknesses they have will be removed and their goodness, too, can emerge. True feelings of friendship really do work in this way.

The architect who built our Global Co-operation House and its extension called the Diamond House in London is an amazing person – he built those buildings in such a way that there is not a single crack in the structures. When there is truth in the work we do, then the value of that truth is such that it becomes a memorial. The reason why it becomes a memorial is because when that work is done with a loving feeling, it creates vibrations and positive energy in that place.

The life of every human being can make a difference – it can provide a support for the whole world. When a person becomes good they make such a difference; not only are they praised, no one is able to forget the memorial of the task they have performed. But to lay a foundation for making a difference to your lives and others, you have to start by going very deep. When you are able to go deep within yourself, the foundation will be so good and strong that a building can be constructed, and that building will last a long time. In that foundation, then, there has to be truth and love. When we begin new ventures with the foundation of love and truth, our characters become very elevated.

In the *Bhagavad Gita*, God and Arjuna have a conversation. It emerges from this that first of all, we should know who we really are; secondly, we should know who God is; and thirdly, we should put great attention on the quality of actions we perform. Whatever actions you perform, do make sure that your conscience is able to guide you – you should be able to think to yourself, 'Yes, this feels right' before starting something. When you do something that feels right, your conscience can be clear. If something doesn't feel right, then make sure you don't allow yourself to do it. When your conscience is clear, you experience the power of the Supreme.

While performing any actions, have faith in God and carry them out with truth in your heart. Also understand that whatever actions you perform, do them not for anyone else, but for your own self. But let the quality of your actions be such that others are inspired to act in a similar way. People study so much in today's world, but the real study should be of the character we build – this is the PhD we have to claim!

The point is that when starting out, your foundation has to be very deep and very strong. You can begin to lay these foundations by going deep into silence. People ask for peace – but there cannot be peace unless you experience silence. To experience silence means going deep inside the self and moving away from external sounds and sights. Even though your eyes are open and you see the scenes outside with your eyes, when you go inside in a state of introversion, you are no longer influenced by them.

We have to go so deep inside to recognise real silence. Then there is only the experience of peace and purity – nothing else. That experience of silence changes into sweet silence and then the experience becomes one of dead silence. When I go deep into that silence, it is as if I go beyond the stars, up into a place like a tower. I go high above. When people speak about God they always point upwards – the One who is the Almighty and who has all powers is also the highest. Then it is as if I receive the rays of the sun and they incinerate all the rubbish so that I am able to experience the light of truth.

So when I go even deeper inside, I move far above, too, and it is through that experience that I come to experience peace, love and power. When I am far away from my attitude and my awareness, the atmosphere becomes very beautiful.

When I go up above and beyond, everything down below is able to sort itself out. I just have to maintain awareness of who am I and what I have to do. Then there is no ego or attachment – there is no awareness of 'I did this' and 'I have got to do that' – there is no worry at all.

This is what you have to do, too. But you will only be able to scale this tower of peace, love and power when you become a tower of purity. And a tower can only stand tall when its foundation is very deep and very strong. You can develop this depth and strength through truth and humility. Inside you there has to be truth and in your relationships with others there has to be humility. And you must have great patience, too; an immense amount of patience. The slightest bit of impatience will leave you peaceless. When we create an atmosphere of peace, deep joy and happiness, we automatically accept each other's ideas. This is what it means to experience the royalty that comes through reality. When we reach that equality, we understand each other's feelings. Let me be my own friend, make God the Supreme my friend, and also maintain the awareness that we are one another's friends.

INSPIRATION

How can we serve those around us?
By making our lives inspirational and interacting with tact and wisdom.

Even if there isn't the chance for actual conversation, we can learn to take in each other's presence in a positive way, honing their goodness and making their specialities our own.

This creates and atmosphere of love and regard, which makes it easy to share spiritual experiences.

We should be so cheerful, and our lives such examples that they say,
'Here is an angel'.

THE SPIRITUAL PATH

A spiritual path is like a school.

Not a regular school where you learn ordinary skills, but a spiritual school where you learn the skills of spirit – like how to remove flaws in your character, or how to remain unaffected by the negative influences around you.

Some people think that if they follow spiritual path, they won't be able to cultivate their individual talents.

However, what kinds of talent do people really need nowadays?

To remove one's own ego is a great talent; to love others is another.

There is no need to study all those other complicated things.

If you have the nature of following God, then God's nature will become your own.

Become true; reveal your true self through your spiritual study, and claim a spiritual degree!

ORIGINAL PEACE

It is not necessary to search for peace; it is within.
Your original state is one of peace.

External situations will pull you away from your peace – that is, if, you let them.
Internal feelings can also pull you away.
Tiredness, for example, leads to irritability.

Learn to be in charge of yourself and maintain your peace: centre your awareness on your spiritual form, a tiny star-like point of light, seated in the middle of your forehead.
Really experience the difference between You the sparkling Star, and your body, the physical vehicle.
Learn to detach yourself from the vehicle.

Even a few moments of this practice, if done regularly, will return you to your natural state of peace.
Tiredness will vanish. Irritability, too.
And your actions will be filled with love – for the self and others.

EARLY MORNING CONTEMPLATION

The best time to dedicate to spiritual progress – whether for prayers, meditation or contemplation – are the early morning hours,.

Having rested through the night, the intellect is fresh and pure.

For expanding your awareness, recognising God and taking a lot of spiritual benefit,

four o'clock in the morning is the best time.

It's an invaluable time for assessing ourselves and seeing how close we've come to self-realisation.

The signs of our progress or slackness are plainly visible.

This meditation reveals to us how much spiritual royalty has been imbibed.

CHILD OF GOD

Do you know yourself as a child of God?

Or are you so overwhelmed by the circumstances of life that you feel you have
not time to be with God?
'There are too many things I have to do,' you say.
This is a perfect example of attachment – to the features of your life;
not to mention your own ego as well.

As an actor on the stage of life you need to detach yourself from the roles you are
playing and get in touch with the part of you that is not an act.

The one experience of 'being' which is not a role, not an act, is 'being the child
of God'.

I am, I have always been and I will always be God's child.
Never doubt this.

There is such strength in this experience; you will easily rise above adversity.
Sorrow will finish and your heart will dance.

Belonging to God fills you with the innocence of a child and the wisdom of God.

SELF-RESPECT

The basis of self-respect is the faith that God loves me.
Through this experience, I will be able to start loving myself.
By studying God's virtues and incorporating them in my daily life, faith in my own inherent worth is enhanced.

It is often difficult to experience self-respect, because my sense of self is usually based on external things – praise, status, income, and so on.
As these fluctuate, so does my self-appreciation.
One day I'll feel there's no one as good as me and the next I'll feel utterly worthless.
Actually, self-respect is not a matter of what I am doing in my life, but rather the degree to which I bring quality and virtue to each act.

SILENCE

There is a part of you that is perfect and pure.
It is untouched by the less than perfect characteristics you've acquired by living in a less than perfect world.

It is filled with divine qualities, so is in a constant state of resourcefulness and well-being.
Its total absence of conflict and negativity of any sort makes this part of you a Still-Point – a deep, enriching experience of silence.

Make time to practise reaching this inner place of silence.
It will bring you untold benefit.

First, it allows you to manage your thoughts better.
You will find, for example, that there is no need to think as much as you do, that much of all that you need will emerge, effortlessly, as you simply sit in silence.

Second, the experience of silence releases you from the grip of your negative programming and conditioning.
You will more easily experience the truth of your inner peace and dignity.
This further aids the mind in remaining focused and capable.

Third, the power of silence can be shared.
As you increase your experience of silence, your power can help those without power to continue in their efforts of self-development and the experience of peace.

Your stock of silence plus an additional stock of true, powerful thought will help others to go beyond the limited into the unlimited and the divine.

It feels so good to 'go beyond' in this way; to leave behind thought and speech and become quiet for a little while.
It's so refreshing and nourishing; it's habit-forming.
Love for spiritual introversion, solitude and silence complements our life in such a beautiful way.

INTROSPECTION

Introspection comes with solitude; the deep and the silent company of God which benefits the soul so profoundly.

Introspection creates the state of poise where I think before I speak.
I don't just speak;
I can put my own nature aside and easily avoid conflict with others.

It does need practice, like speaking only when necessary and putting an end to excuses
about never having the time.

With introspection, I can take charge of my mind, purify the intellect and change any habit I want to.
Spirituality then takes root and I am transformed.

CHEERFULNESS

Inner cheer is destroyed by a conscience which bites, so learn to do everything in a worthwhile way.
It's an art which teaches you to appreciate your inner beauty.
(It makes you think twice about ruining it, too).

We used to be hard on ourselves when we made a mistake.
It's much more effective to be handled with love.
Telling the self off is a terrible habit; it subtly shapes a nature of sorrow.

Finish the business of thinking rubbish and instead take delight in all that you've found.

TOLERANCE

Tolerance is based on going beyond the superficial things that divide us.
It's the result of turning within and coming to know the Self.
If I can deal with my own ego, then my own anger can be resolved.
This goes a long way in resolving external issues, too.
With my own ego out of the way, I will be able to handle anything!
Otherwise, it's just the same old thing – you versus me, yours versus mine –
intolerance.

If I'm unselfish and honest in my heart, and am concerned about others' needs,
then I will be full enough to give.
When you know the self in this way, then you can know others.
'I should be understood' changes to 'I should understand'.
Not, 'They should change', but 'I will give what's needed'.
Patience, peace and maturity develop.
Spiritual tolerance cultivates inner wisdom, the kind you can't get from books.

Turn within and in silence fill yourself with your Godly inheritance.
Always remember, you don't have to prove anything.
Whatever is true is going to be revealed, anyway.
Working to win the hearts of others is what will bring happiness to your life.

SPIRITUAL TOLERANCE

Tolerance does not mean to simply leave a thing as it is – the 'grin and bear it' attitude of the world.

Spiritual tolerance enables you to stay within a crisis and help to resolve it, because tolerance is of a higher order, or higher power, than ego or anger.

It means you are able to respond with understanding, care and compassion to the situation.

Where there are feelings of friendship and love, difficulties will be overcome.

To tolerate something is a demonstration of goodwill, of having the aim to be co-operative and work for resolution.

Tolerance wins the heart of others.

FAITH IN OTHERS

If there is a need to take responsibility for something, then of course you should. However, if a situation is not your business, or someone else is in charge, then don't get caught up in it.

If you want to help, you can still involve yourself in a more subtle way – through faith.

Faith in others does a lot of work. It doesn't mean blind faith – observing helplessly while keeping your fingers crossed – it means to remain alert to what's going on, and then to fill another with the strength of your faith to such an extent that they feel able to do whatever needs to be done.

This means having faith, but also donating the power of your faith.

If the other person is honest and truthful, your faith will work for them.

In this way, we can learn to truly help each other.

RESPECT FOR OTHERS

Respect for others is the result of spiritual awareness.
With spiritual awareness, I recognise the efforts of those around me to improve themselves. This encourages me to focus more on the potential and unique specialities of my companions, rather than on their faults.
In fact, this is the method to help people to be free of their faults.

I can judge the quality of my spiritual awareness by seeing how much faith I have in the ultimate transformation of my companions.
This faith and love is true respect.

CO-OPERATION

Co-operation is based on four specific things:

First of all, constant pure feelings and elevated motives.
If you aren't careful about cultivating the right kind of feelings in every moment, your nature will suffer.

Secondly, faith in God.
Ego is cultivated when you don't understand that it is God who is doing everything. This ego creates competition and jealousy.

Thirdly, trust in your colleagues and those who are close.
This faith in others creates enthusiasm, which further serves to increase self-confidence.

Finally, constant communication of your motives, using easy and simple language. This makes it possible for everyone to understand, and feel a part of the whole.

PATIENCE

The most important virtue needed for self-transformation is patience.
Without patience you will lose hope in the transformation process.

As you travel the path you sometimes run into rough spots where your foot slips
and you find yourself suddenly not on the path, and there are wrong thoughts
or words or behaviour.

Patience makes you cool and calm; It makes the journey possible.

The process of self-realisation is not a ten-yard dash; it is the one-hundred-and-
fifty-mile run.
You have to learn to pace yourself.
Patience teaches you to pace yourself.

You can't take help from God until there is patience of this kind.
Where there is patience, there is peace.
Where there is peace, there is love.
This is a whole new experience of what it means to be human.

HUMILITY

Humility comes from understanding that the force behind whatever help you give to others comes not from you but from the power of love.

It is not true that if you are humble others will walk all over you.

It is when there is no humility that you can be easily influenced by others and things seem difficult.

But when there is humility, there is also the power of truth.

You know internally that you will achieve your aim, regardless of what others say or think.

A humble person never feels that they are bowing to others. The head is held neither high nor low – it just faces straight ahead, like an angel.

Humility reveals your truth.

Ego makes you criticise others and get caught up in a web.

Ego puts a lock on the intellect, obscuring your own responsibility.

Ego makes you say: 'This is your fault, it has nothing to do with me.'

Humility is the key to this lock. It frees you from self-deception.

Humility allows you to hear and obey your conscience.

With humility there is the power of realisation, which allows transformation to take place; the soul can recognise a mistake in a second.

It's easy to settle any argument quickly. You are able to say: 'Okay, I'm wrong...'

Humility makes the heart honest, big and clean. It enables you to be cooperative and have easy relationships with everyone.

Humility enables you to win God's heart, the hearts of others and even your own heart!

Inner conflict with your own feelings finishes, so confusion and difficulties also end.

There is contentment, faith and the feeling of love for everyone.

HONESTY

Spiritual honesty means, 'To thine own self, be true'.

It is one of the pillars of greatness, as it evokes a practical experience of God's love, and the feeling that God and I are very close.

There is so much power in this experience.

Unfortunately, instead of enjoying such greatness in a natural way, most people forgo this opportunity by making excuses.

Lying is an obvious form of dishonesty, but in fact making excuses is worse.

While falsehoods are usually easily detected, it can be a long time before we realise that we are making excuses.

A lot of life can be wasted by this deception.

When you think about it, what excuse could there be for not making yourself close to God?

THE DRAMA OF LIFE

Every passing moment is like a passing act in a play.
Each of us are the actors playing our parts very well.

An actor is never focused on another actor's part, continually criticising it.
He just gets on with his part, playing it as best he can.

This drama of life is eternal, predestined and accurate.
Whatever anybody else says or does is their role, not mine.
My task is to play my part right.
Right thoughts restore rightness to the whole play.

Practise detaching yourself from your role and experiencing the truth behind
the role and you will find yourself loving every instant of your role, and the
drama, too.

And the question, 'Why has this happened?' will be answered.

PLAYING YOUR PART

Never have the thought that you do not want a part in the Drama of Life – that is not possible.

It is good to understand these things in detail; understanding allows you to remove the sorrow – it makes you self-sovereign and makes others this, too.

What is needed is to prepare the self internally for whatever scene may come. Attention to the self like this removes all worry and concern.

Then, even extreme situations appear as side scenes – they will come and they will go.

Your mind will stay free, happy and powerful, and this is what you'll share with others.

THE SPIRITUAL ARMY

Against the forces of falsehood and evil, the spiritual army is now being shaped.
The forces of evil are all forms of negativity.
What do you have to do in order to be a good spiritual soldier?

First of all, don't be afraid. Although these forces of negativity are within the self
as well as in the world, faith in your ultimate victory will give you the strength
to face all challenges.

Secondly, pay attention to becoming virtuous, not just to remaining peaceful.
Also, stay alert. Alertness is probably the most important characteristic of a
successful warrior.
Everything within an army depends on alertness – promotion, progress, victory
and defeat.

If a soldier is not alert, he'll be dismissed.
Spiritual alertness will help you to recognise negativity as soon as it comes up.
Finally, if even only one soul remains alert, there is then safety for many others.

PART 2

THE JOURNEY CONTINUES – TALKING TO THE SELF

DADI'S FIRST THOUGHTS...

LOVE IS connected to virtues. Virtues create love both within the self and within others. When virtues reduce, the quality of love also reduces. When all virtues are present, there is complete and pure love.

Out of all the virtues, the main virtue is honesty. If we feel someone is not being honest with us, our love breaks. Whether it is our mother, father, husband, wife or friend, if we feel that they are being dishonest, love breaks. In terms of our relationship with God, if we are honest with God we will draw His love. If we are not, that love will break. Even if we have no other virtue than this one of honesty, we will be able to draw God's love.

So see the importance of being honest.

The first kind of honesty is honesty with myself. If I am honest with myself, there need be no situation in which I am not honest with others. If someone does not believe me, if someone distrusts my honesty, perhaps it is a sign that I need to become more honest. Instead of blaming them, I should realise this, and look at how to become more honest.

Honesty does not mean simply speaking our mind. Honesty means to be very clear about everything going on inside us. Where there is honesty, feelings become pure and clean. Honesty is where there are no other thoughts or feelings inside, other than those that God Himself would have.

Such clarity is reflected in our words; they will be filled with the power of truth, and spoken with ease and without hesitation. The genuine honesty cultivated within us is what will reach out and touch others.

Being easily influenced by people will diminish our ability to remain honest. Others will not be able to get that feeling of truth from us, and our interactions will not carry a feeling of love. They will seem superficial. Although superficial love is better than no love at all – at least it ensures that we don't become completely dry – it will nonetheless be obvious that it is not the real thing.

God is teaching us the art of loving. He is the Bestower, He is the Ocean of Love and He is willing to give us so much. But first we have to learn the art of detachment, otherwise we won't have the right to claim His love.

Detachment is a talent as well as an art. It is developed through soul-consciousness which, together with a deep relationship with God, will keep us from being deceived by the attraction of limited love. It means to be so centred in the consciousness of our true spiritual nature that there is a natural, automatic rejection of adverse personality traits within us and illusionary attraction around us. Detachment allows us to be unaffected by these and so able to continue cultivating the values and virtues of our spiritual personality.

God is willing to give us all His love, but if the first condition of detachment is not met we will not be able to receive it. Turning our eyes in any other direction will block the truth and finish our progress. It's a very strong prerequisite.

Until we learn how to detach ourselves from a limited consciousness, human love, with all its limitations, will attract us against our will again and again. Detachment of this sort is cultivated by reaching for God in such a way that we feel Him satisfying the needs of any and all relationships. God is the Ocean of Love, so it is possible to experience Him as our perfect Father, Mother, Beloved, and so on, all at the same time. It is only when we expose ourselves to all the aspects of God's love that we are then purified- that is- made full by its power. A limited consciousness will not allow us to experience such fullness.

Only by being faithful to One can we fulfil ourselves in this way. Souls have the habit of being distracted by the physical world. We have to study and look after ourselves to ensure that this does not happen to us. The only thing that will break this habit is the practice of soul-consciousness. By being introverted, by turning our attention to One, we will continue to receive light and might from God.

People tend to gravitate towards whatever produces an experience of love. We are drawn in that direction and often get stuck there. We form an attachment and this continues to suck us in. I was never attracted towards anyone or anything in this way. And I have always rejected the kind of love that some people offer after conferring some status or title.

I don't think I have ever run after anyone's love – not even at the point of my greatest spiritual search. I never expected it from my father, my mother, my husband, my guru, or my friends; not from anyone. I always did have, however, a very deep desire to experience the love of God.

People started prayer and worship in the hope of receiving something from God; we had a pull, or desire, to experience the love of God. The experience of perfect love is deep within our subconscious personality and, because we had this experience at some point, we have been searching for it ever since. It is exactly because of this deep inner experience that we will always be dissatisfied with any kind of false love.

Although false love might work for a little while, ultimately we will always feel that something is missing and that what we are experiencing is not true, real love. So the search is then taken up once again. Our search for perfect love eventually pulls us back to finding and experiencing the love of God.

When we embark upon a spiritual path, we automatically receive a lot of love from God in order to gain the power to free ourselves from other limited supports. We are like little babies who don't need to do anything in order to receive that love. But then, as we continue on the path, growing older and stronger, God wants to teach us how to use our own head. So He stands back and watches: is the child following His teachings properly; is the child observing spiritual principles? He watches to see whether we study well and change, or whether we become lazy or careless in the study.

If I am not studying properly, I lose my right to that love. The love will be there, but I will no longer be able to connect to it. If I don't study properly – if there has been no integration of spiritual understandings into my everyday, practical life – how much further will I be able to go? I won't be making my life good, so what goodness will I have to share with others? How can I be an inspiration to make the lives of others good? God gives special love to those children who are ready to help. If I don't study, how can God give me that love?

Learning the art of true, Godly love is a feature of transcendence. It is like ascending to the very peak of a mountain. At the bottom, at the beginning of the journey, it doesn't matter so much if we misplace our footing and slip – it won't be that dangerous. But the higher we go, the narrower the path. If we slip while higher up, we will hurt ourselves a hundredfold.

If we find that the laws governing our spiritual progress are too strict, this can only be because we have not yet understood nor truly experienced God's love. People do not surrender themselves to God on the basis of spiritual knowledge, but rather because of their attraction to God's love. We experience the honesty in His love, and this makes us believe that our life here and now can become honest and good. Understanding comes later; the laws come later. The first experience is love. For this to happen, I simply allow myself to be the child again. God is happy to take me into His lap with the unlimited, unconditional love of the perfect Parent.

QUALITY OF THOUGHTS

An enlightened person understands that there is nothing to be gained by thinking about others.
Pure thoughts and feelings will do all the work; there's no need to think any further.

The quality of your thoughts will affect your spiritual endeavour, so keep checking them.
If you don't, then at some point your mode of thinking will become quite ordinary, no longer spiritual.
The sign of this is that your mind begins to race and you start reacting sensitively to little things; you become vulnerable not just to the opinions of others, but even to your own (limited) way of understanding.

Thoughts can be your own best friend, or worst enemy.
It's up to you.

COURAGE

You need courage to remain true to yourself in today's artificial world.
This is not a small thing

However, the very purpose of a spiritual journey is to restore courage – the courage to stand for what you believe in.

Your original, true nature is of peace and divinity.
To experience this is to be convinced of the absolute value of your intrinsic worth.
You can face any opposition with the strength of your convictions.

Many people have difficulty believing in their higher self;
others simply no longer believe in the future.

Self-realisation removes doubts:
My original nature is peace.
I am not a slave to my personality traits
(I am their creator).
I am a spectator as well as an actor in the drama of life.
Whatever is happening is beneficial

As you incorporate these truths into your life, your courage will never fail.

DETACHMENT

You need power to remain free from the influence of others.
Detachment is the power.
If you can't stay detached from the influences, you will not be able to keep your thoughts under control.
From there it will be a downward spiral until all trace of inner well-being is lost.

The first step in detachment is to understand who you are as a spiritual entity.
This allows you to 'detach' yourself from your physical identity, and its world of limited thoughts and feelings, and 'attach' instead to your spiritual personality, the being of inner peace and power.

A normal day will be filled with challenges to this detachment.
On the one side will be your spiritual awareness, but on the other will be the attraction towards human beings and the material world.
Detachment is not a question of becoming separate from the latter, but of simply remaining conscious of yourself as a spiritual being and playing your part in the world.
Detachment simply means to keep yourself centred in your spirituality.

STRENGTH

Spiritual strength is necessary if you want to grow spiritually and help others grow, too.
It's an inner kind of strength which builds character and allows you to discipline your mind.
A disciplined mind means a peaceful and happy one.
A strong mind never gets disturbed.

To develop this strength, cultivate honesty and deep love and regard for God.
This will allow you to protect yourself from being negatively influenced by your surroundings – both physical and emotional.

Blessings from others are another source of strength for the self.
Blessings come to you from those you have served, and a very good way to serve others is to share this kind of inner strength.
Those who have incorporated God's virtues in their outlook and activities are the ones who can give strength to others.
To give guidance and wisdom like this means to give the gift of life.

PURITY

A powerful, yet often misunderstood aim of spiritual study is purity.
Purity of the soul means a return to its original divine qualities.
The soul has become so polluted with less than divine qualities that it can hardly enjoy being alive.
Purifying the soul puts the higher self back in charge – useless and negative thoughts are removed and annoying habits finish.
A pure soul cannot be touched by sorrow; indeed, the power of purity is such that it serves to remove the sorrow of the whole world.
Purity restores happiness – even bliss.

All you need to do, in order to re-establish your purity, is to want this.
But you need to want it intensely, to the exclusion of everything else.
The one thought, 'I must become completely pure', sparks a fire of love between you and God. This fire melts away all the pollution, and your purity becomes such a power that it frees you from all battles forever, making you a true and eternal companion of God.

SELF-AWARENSS

A beautiful state of being is soul-consciousness, where your whole sense of self is shifted from a physical identity to a spiritual one.
In soul-consciousness, you no longer feel yourself to be male or female, black or white.
No worldly achievement forms your self-esteem. Instead, self-esteem is shaped by a deep, abiding experience of your intrinsic worth as a child of God.

A lack of soul-consciousness puts your well-being at the mercy of your environment – you become a slave to the influences of the people and situations around you – feeling happy and good only when outside events warrant it.
This kind of dependency leaves the soul weak and confused.
Soul-consciousness, on the other hand, frees you from external influences, allowing you to create an inner well-being which is totally independent.

Soul-consciousness is cultivated through deliberate practice, and only those who have understood the need for this kind of true, inner self-respect will make the effort.
Difficulties will arise to test your resolve for self-upliftment – physical illness, relationships, memories of the past, and so on.
Yet with patience and introspection, you will come to see how these very tests are the means to strengthen your spiritual identity.

ACCOMPLISHMENT

～

Spiritual accomplishment means:
you are fully centred in your spiritual identity,
you know yourself as a child of God,
the present is fully experienced, the past completely finished and the future clearly understood.

Spiritual accomplishment is received from God.
A distracted intellect will not be able to turn towards God and receive.
It will be too busy thinking 'How?' and 'Why?' and turning to the world for understanding, which only serves to divert the intellect even more.
It's a lack of faith which destroys spiritual progress.

So don't be distracted; rather, tolerate and persevere and you'll be able to receive everything that God is giving.

LEADING OTHERS

Good leadership is based on skills which are incognito, like pure feelings, faith and trust.
These keep both your frame of mind and the task moving in the right direction.

It is human to err, but your high hopes for someone can actually eliminate errors.
Doubting people has exactly the opposite effect.

Believing in someone, extending feelings of trust, never telling people what to do, but stepping aside and watching, with faith, this is what enables a task to get done in the right way.

Spiritual skills like these are cultivated by avoiding complacency, learning to be sensitive and staying alert.
Also, keep an eye on your own spiritual health.
Don't look to others for whatever is lacking, look within, see what remains to be done and do it.
Never allow those with strong personalities to tell you what to do, especially when you feel something else to be right.
This creates depression and you can't afford to be disheartened.

Take care of yourself with understanding and love and make sure that you never compromise your own spiritual growth.

WOMEN AS SERVERS

The idea of women playing any role outside the home was strongly opposed in the community where I grew up. That was a long time ago and things have changed. But I didn't wait for the change. I had the strong desire to work for the upliftment of humanity, and that's what I set out to do.

The courage to do this came from being very clear about my spiritual identity. In point of fact, I am neither male nor female. I am soul, the child of God, currently inside a female form. I was also very clear about my aim, and concerned about how to be of more service to others.

The world has never looked to women for help in solving its problems. Instead it has turned to those of great authority, to scholars and to the very wealthy. This has been the crucial mistake.

The mother's role is to awaken the children with great love and prepare them for the rest of the day. She is their support. She nurtures.

Generally it is attachment to the home and children which prevents women from fulfilling their unlimited calling. To go beyond that attachment is no small accomplishment. To go beyond the fear of what society will say is no less.

My relationships with God gave me such internal power that I was not intimidated by social convention. The spirit was strong and so withstood all external pressures and influences.

SUBTLE SERVICE

Your pure vibrations are a subtle form of service.

Love, peace, joy, wisdom – these are pure vibrations.
They are carried out into the world through your thoughts and actions whenever these are filled with the Divine.

So make your every moment pure: understand the difference between the ordinary and the Divine, then put the Divine alone into practice.
Remember that you are master of both your mind and body, then give your commands and keep them in order.
As you learn how to tell your mind what to do, old ways of thinking and doing will change.

As the master of both your mind and body you will see things not as they appear, but as they truly are.
You react less, respond more.

Your very presence becomes an invitation to truth. Your vibrations reach out, bringing coolness and peace – words wouldn't be even half as effective. The help is extended through your state of mind.

And everyone is benefited, not just those around you, but all your brothers and sisters, all over the whole world.

PURE THOUGHTS

You are what you think.

Love, purity, peace, wisdom – the more you think of these things, the more you will become them.

Weakness – blown out of proportion in yourself or in others – invites negative thinking. This will destroy you.

Learn how to shift your focus.
Instead think: though I am not yet pure, I want purity.
God is leading me to my destination, so I will definitely become pure.

When you build a house, every brick counts.
When you build a character, every thought counts.

I will not become pure unless I think about it first.

MAKING PEACE

There is something that you can do to help create peace in the world, and that is to make yourself peaceful.

The first step in this is doing some real soul-searching to find out what has made you peace-less in the first place. Turning your mind within allows you to discover, underneath the many-surfaced emotions of everyday life, a deep undisturbed pool of spiritual well-being. You need to explore that part of the self, not just to understand it, but to experience it, again and again.

This is a very satisfying experience, one that refreshes the soul and fills it with peace. From this vantage point, it becomes easy to recognise the kind of thoughts and feelings which are self-destructive. The power of self-realisation will work wonders in transforming these destructive mental habits. You will stop blaming others for your peacelessness, and get on with the work of cultivating your truth.

Peace is made up of many things: love, patience, wisdom.

You should not be content with just a little of it, but fill yourself completely. As you practice putting these into your interactions with others, your very nature will become peaceful.

This proves to be of benefit not only to yourself, but to all those around you as well. Thus you are becoming a helper in world transformation. It isn't enough for you simply to be peaceful. You must spread the waves and create an atmosphere of peace through your thoughts, words and interactions with others.

Ours is a peace-less world. Only when you truly adopt your original religion of peace can you hope to bring peace to the world.

RELIGION

I used to say, 'I am a Hindu,
You are a Christian'.

I could never say that anymore.
My attitude has changed.
Now I would say, 'Whether you're standing before a statue of Christ or worshipping the image of Krishna,
God is still the one Father and we are all the children of the one Father'.

Religion no longer exists in the world in a true form.
When merely ritualistic, it is superficial and without power.

Where there is real understanding, where there is truth in words, there is also power.

Power would not be received from God in order for us to fight each other.
Power is received for us to become peaceful.

True religion says, 'Peace'.
True religion teaches peace.

STAYING PEACEFUL

I have faith that the force of peace is greater than the atomic bomb, greater than any power the world can produce.

All of us need to put our faith in this force;
Not, 'I'll just keep my gun handy', or,
'We'll just keep these bombs handy... in case they are needed', but, 'I trust absolutely in this power'.

I was once asked how I could stay so peaceful trying to teach peace to so many different kinds of people.

I just keep my aim in front of me: to stay full of peace myself, knowing this peace will reach my beloved ones and, ultimately, the whole world.

TALKING TO THE SELF

When you talk to yourself in your mind, which self do you address?
And how? Usually people do not talk to their divinity, but to the most superficial aspect of their everyday personality.
And often it's a stream of fears, complaints and a mindless repetition of old things.
If we talked that way to another human being, we would have to apologise.

Learning to talk properly to the self is a spiritual endeavour.
Thoughts from the past and worries about the future do not create good conversation.
Instead learn to talk to your mind as if it were a child.
Talk to it with love.
If you just force a child to sit down, he won't.
A good mother knows how to prompt her child into doing what she wants.
Be a good mother to your mind; teach it good, positive thoughts so that when you tell it sit quietly, it will.
Love your mind. Stay happy.

RULER OF THE SELF

There is a connection between a mind which is peaceful and behaviour which is good.
It is interesting to note how the sensory apparatus – sight, touch, hearing, taste and smell – are all involved in this.

For example, suppose I promise myself not to get angry anymore, but then later in the day I see or hear something negative.
If I allow myself to forget my promise – that is, if my level of awareness regresses to what it was before my promise – then my immediate reaction will probably be one that is equally negative.
However, if I remember my promise, the same stimuli will most likely produce a wiser, more resourceful response.

With spiritual study, my mind grows strong in its commitment to peace and truth in action.
This strength allows me to gain control over the sense organs.
I simply don't allow them to take in whatever they want, according to any of my old habits.
I remain consciously present, monitoring whatever they do.
It is the first step in becoming a master
– ruler of the Kingdom of the Self.

LEARNING

Some things facilitate learning, and other things destroy it.
Arrogance destroys it.
'I know this already': have this thought and learning will stop.

Also, being tied up in a million things will not help you get to the depth of a thing.
And you can't really change until you get to the depth of something.

When learning stops, there is no more change, there is no more progress and the soul, whose task it is to learn and change, is bereft.

'This much I have understood, but tomorrow I will understand even more': this thought is a thought of appreciation for what has already been received.
It is a good way to ensure that more will be received in the future.

There will always be the opportunity to learn for those who desire it.
Learn in such a way so as to absorb the new and live it.
That's being sensible, which is the aim of learning.

SUCCESS

Success means to reach such a constant level of positive thoughts that pure actions happen naturally. Pure actions are like good seeds which, when planted, produce healthy, sweet fruit.

'As you sow, so shall you reap'.
Concern for the quality of my actions today ensures the success of my tomorrow. Virtues are the mainstay in this because success like this requires hope, and hope, in today's world, requires courage. It is a matter of working from the strength of your convictions, which is a spiritual kind of honesty.

Balance these qualities and your path will be easy. You will only move forward. Your success will be assured.

Courage alone does not bring success. If there's only courage, there will be ego. It's courage plus honesty which brings God's help and that is what guarantees success.

'God is getting it done through me',
'I am simply an instrument in this task':
these are honest thoughts which elicit God's help and protection.

Humility is the result of such honesty and courage.
A life of enthusiasm, courage, honesty and humility is inspirational.
It's a way of helping others become successful, too.

PART 3

OVERCOMING OBSTACLES ON THE PATH

DADI'S FIRST THOUGHTS...

⌒〜

WE BEGAN to descend from our spiritual heights when we started using the body in the wrong way. We are souls, and we begin a cycle of birth and rebirth upon taking a physical body. Eventually we begin to use the body for vice and from that time onwards, a lot of rubbish starts to accumulate in the soul. This is how we lost our peace, happiness, love and purity. All the negative things, which have affected us in this lifetime and those gone by, have penetrated deeply within the soul. It is nothing ordinary to eliminate them all.

We start by eliminating the obvious vices: dependencies such as tobacco, alcohol, lust. But the real effort is in removing the subtle vices, like ego. The subtle vices do not allow us to feel we belong to God.

The difficulty with ego is that it is deeply concealed. Most of us don't even know we have it. Saying something to us about it just increases our arrogance. Ego destroys love. It destroys the ability to learn, so there is no more give and take. I go through many kinds of situations all day long and I make sure I don't stop exchanging love.

Ego can be overcome by developing humility. There should be as much humility in the soul as there is honesty so that the more honest we become, the greater the humility we have. Both go together. If we know how to bow, there will be love. If we don't know how to bow, love finishes. We have to bow down again and again. Bow, bow, bow.

The secret behind this is never to stop the give and take of love with God. In this way, we can make our heart so strong that we are no longer able to be hurt by anything. Hurt feelings are the main reason why we the give and take of love stops.

Most people don't understand themselves. There isn't the patience to understand themselves or others. We need to make time for this. We get too impatient. Very often, because we are not willing to take this time, misunderstandings continue. We don't take the time to listen to someone quietly and try to understand them. Then we start inventing things about them, because we simply haven't taken the time to understand.

To focus solely on myself, without any concern for what is happening to others, reflects a weakness in my effort. Cultivating humility will allow souls to come close. From there I need to balance maintaining a certain formality or quietness – so that relationships don't become too casual or familiar – and giving love, with ease and lightness.

Right now, what the soul really needs most is power. Having been through birth and rebirth, accumulating rubbish along the way, the soul is burdened and depleted and therefore unable to perform to its greatest potential. Power is gained, enabling us to stay with God and reach the destination, when we use our inner resources in the right way. Wasting the mind on ordinary mundane, conditioned thinking is a waste of time and energy. Souls leave the path; they leave God, because they have wasted their thoughts, words and breath in this way. Blaming others and complaining are just making excuses. This is another mistake which wastes more energy and causes more loss of power. There isn't time to behave in this way anymore. Understand that we need power and start cultivating it. As power develops, so will love.

People have experienced a lot of deception in their lives. There has been a lot of exchange of everything that is false, so feelings have been destroyed. This is why some people have stopped feeling altogether, and have rejected the world. However, when a soul starts receiving something from God the heart opens up. So let us take God's love and have pure feelings. Let us experience what pure feelings are. Let us have trust in each other and faith in ourselves. Let us learn to love ourselves. Let there be purity in our feelings, so that we can then experience love. Let us take from God and give to others. When we have very powerful good wishes and feelings for others, those feelings reach them. We can help each other through the power of our good feelings.

Deep in my heart there is just this one feeling: just as I have received so much from God, may all God's children receive the same from our One and only Father.

OBSTACLES ON THE PATH

Obstacles are inevitable, so don't get upset.
Any form of worry erodes your strength.

Never see a situation as difficult.
Never ask, 'Why has this happened?'
Never feel you are on your own.

Remember, God is always with you.
God is giving you support.

Take time to go into silence.
Silence stops confusion.
Your power will be restored.

Many obstacles occur because of your own mistakes.
Don't become someone else's obstacle because of your own.

OBSTACLES WITHIN

A major obstacle to spiritual progress is one's own negative nature.
The root cause of this kind of nature is limited consciousness.
This root has to be eliminated completely because obstacles that arise from a negative nature will prevent you from taking power from God.

Power from God is received through the awareness and faith that God belongs to you.
A negative nature could destroy even this faith.

Recognising the root of the problem helps to transform it.
Limited thinking should simply not be tolerated.
There should be total cleanliness inside. For this you need to be very honest about the obstacles you are facing, because it is easy to deceive yourself.

Limited thinking will be transformed when you spend time in the awareness of your true nature of peace and in being of help to others.

PROBLEM-SOLVING

The trick to problem-solving is to get to the root of a problem before it even shows up.

This requires virtues such as objectivity, clarity and honesty, because the solution to all problems is truth.

Truth means your spirituality; that is, your essence – the way something is before attitudes and opinions are added.

This truth will bring you closer to God, and His pure influence will allow you to perceive the essence of any problem easily.

Working on a problem at the level of its essence is a beautiful experience.

This beauty has a transformative effect, not just on you and the problem, but also on the ones who cause the problems.

Every day you should ask yourself how much you have thought of yourself in your essenceful form, that is, as a spiritual being, an eternal child of the Divine.

This is the method to increase not just your awareness, but your spiritual beauty as well.

This makes problem-solving easy.

FRIENDS AND RELATIONS

If my friends and relations do not choose to accompany me on my spiritual path, why should I chase after them trying to get them to change?

They won't listen to me anyway, no matter what I say.

A better approach is to focus on my own change process.

A river doesn't need to urge people into drinking its water. People are naturally drawn to it, provided its waters are pure, free-flowing and sweet.

In the same way, become so attractive through your spiritual efforts that everyone will want to join you, naturally.

We are hindered in this by attachments, which tend to make us forget that our well-being is not dependent on others at all, that we each have the capacity to flow and sparkle in our own unique way.

Having forgotten this, we developed the habit of turning to others to feel good about ourselves. Using other people in this way is a deceptive source of well-being, and this deception leads to a great deal of pain.

We can change this habit by keeping an eye on our aim. If we don't, our spiritual powers will be destroyed again and again as we allow ourselves to come under the influence of limited emotions.

Instead of losing out like this, we should pay more attention to what we are doing.

We will only be able to make others free when we free ourselves first.

COMPARISON WITH OTHERS

Comparing your progress in self-development with that of others will leave you vulnerable on three counts:

you'll either feel inferior, superior, or impressed.

All three of these states are dangerous because they disregard the underlying principle of our true connection with each other – mutual love and regard, based on independently generated self-esteem.

To protect yourself from this vulnerability, make sure that your attention remains turned within, towards the spiritual experience of pure pride.

Staying centred in your elevated self-respect will help you remain undisturbed by others around you.

Keep asking yourself, 'Who am I?' 'How would my spiritual personality respond to this event or person?'

This will help to centre you further, and allow you to enjoy the successful efforts of others.

INFLUENCES

Let me be humble and let me harmonise and work well with all others,
but let me not become like them.

Others may be influenced by their own arrogance,
or by their own negativities, or by ordinariness in the mind,
but this does not mean that I have to be.

There should be so much truth in me that others become truthful.

My inner state should be such that not only am I not influenced by the negativity
of others, but my very presence is a positive influence on all negativities.
This is true, spiritual detachment.

It is so exhilarating to experience yourself as a spiritual being.
You should never hide that sparkle on the face that comes from having come to
God.

Everything we used to do on the basis of ego can now be done out of love.

FRIENDSHIP

Friendships on the spiritual path require caution, if we are to enjoy them fully. Sometimes we get so involved in our relationships that our own individual spiritual progress in undermined.

This is a mistake, because the very purpose of friendship is to uplift, and if I am remiss in my spiritual efforts, I will not be able to exert the positive influence of my own most elevated state.

One should always maintain the intention of being of help to friends. But that help needs to be devoid of any desire for praise, and above any reactions of ill-feeling or sorrow. Offering this kind of help, will only further my spiritual growth.

If, on the other hand, my offer is tainted, 99 per cent of its sweetness will be removed, and people will notice this.

In fact, it's the sweetness which creates spiritual friendships, the willingness to listen and learn from each other, in order to grow.

RELATIONSHIPS

When a relationship is not working, it is usually because there are needs and expectations that are not being met.
There might be so much anger or hatred that your only desire might be just to run away from it all.
However, this is not a solution! It merely reflects your lack of understanding about where the real problem lies.

The root of all needs and expectations is an unfulfilled spiritual desire.
Satisfy your spiritual desires through the practice of meditation and you will be able to interact successfully with anyone.
No longer needy, you will enter into relationships simply to share and enjoy.
There'll be no strings attached in the way you give of yourself; your love will be unconditional.

We must learn to bring spirituality into our relationships.
Others will learn by our example.
It's a way of inspiring and uplifting each other.

EMOTIONAL PAIN

In a situation of emotional distress, you usually have two options:
to face the problem, or not.
Processing the problem means you are facing it.
Suppressing the problem means you are not.
There's a big difference between the two.

Processing is to the mind what digesting is to the stomach.
If your digestive system can't handle certain food, you have to stop eating them,
otherwise you become sick.
Similarly, if you find yourself in a situation where you can't cope, don't just sit
there taking it all in. It's better to say something right there and then.
To hold something inside will not allow you to have a healthy mind.
What you take in will be indigestible and it will be obvious to others that you are
having a problem.

Our ability to cope is hampered by thinking too much about other people. This
causes problems in the mental digestive system.
The best mental 'antacid' is in-depth spiritual study. This, plus a regular practice
of self-awareness, penetrates the mind very deeply, dislodging emotional pain
at its roots.
Only then can emotion be purified, refined, and ultimately transformed.

CALMING THE MIND

Don't give your mind permission to get disturbed. A disturbed mind is easily influenced.
This will cost you your peace.
Learn to maintain your peace by freeing yourself from attachments.

Competing or comparing yourself with others will not allow you to focus inwards.
An inner focus allows you to keep your eye on your higher self and remember your original nature.
It allows you to forge a link with the Divine. Then it becomes easy to recognise useless thoughts and replace them with a spiritual perspective.

Introversion replaces inner sorrow with praise for God.
You feel delight. You feel renewed.

God is teaching us how to turn within, so listen very carefully.

Keep a check on yourself and change. Don't wait for others to say something

A calm mind is not just peaceful, it is focused, self-directing and divine.

THE BENEFIT OF SICKNESS

Being sick is an opportunity to experience yourself in a new way.
Do you understand and accept this opportunity readily? Or are you unable to take advantage of it, too distracted by the illness?
If that is the case, then you need to take a closer look at yourself, to see where another kind of sickness might lie.

Just as the outward cure for sickness involves going to a hospital, seeing a doctor, getting a comfortable bed and eating healthy food, the internal cure is the same.
I need to go to the Soul World, where the Supreme Doctor resides, rest in the comfortable bed of His remembrance, and eat the nourishing food of pure and positive thoughts.

Sickness is the chance to teach the mind to remain independent of the physical state and so connect with your inner resources of peace and silence.
This is the ultimate cure.

UNDERSTANDING SICKNESS

A spiritual attitude towards sickness is to see it is as a result of your own past actions.

This is due to the law of karma, which states that whatever your situation is today,

it is the result of what you did yesterday.

These actions may have been performed in the immediate past, or the far distant one. If you can accept responsibility in this way and your heart knows how to stay in the remembrance of God, then you will gain such power that even a major physical illness will not affect your ability to cope. Mountains are reduced to molehills.

Without proper understanding, the reverse is true and even a tiny physical complaint seems like something enormous.

Spiritual understanding teaches you how to perform actions so as to guarantee yourself a healthy future. It makes you realise the importance of performing good actions, as these result in a good future. For example, you can bring a lot of subtle energy and strength to yourself if you engage your body, mind and wealth in the service of humanity. An adverse effect, on the other hand, is produced when these same things are used in a negative way.

PHYSICAL PAIN

It is possible to experience so much love from God that whatever pain you have, you will no longer feel it.
Experience Him as the Mother and let Him soothe it away in a second, as you sit on His lap.

It's much better than crying (which doesn't work anyway), and also, it's a spiritual victory.

Be tolerant with pain. It's trying to teach you something.
Don't look at the illness; see the lesson instead.

Remembrance of God is a quality cure.
Understand the relationship of happiness to pain.
It's a magician; it makes it disappear.

So detach yourself from the body in the firm faith of God, and the pain will finish, very quickly.

SPIRITUAL HEALTH

Good spiritual health means I am free from the diseases of the spirit.
No traces of negativity remain.
All obstacles have been overcome.
My face sparkles with happiness.

Good spiritual health comes from a healthy spiritual birth.
Be born to your true self – the Personality of Purity – by remembering God, your eternal parent.

I am living my life with God.
I am talking to God.
I am learning from God.

Inner joy is the best medicine.
It all depends on what you hold in your heart.

SPIRITUAL MEDICINE

The mind has an influence on the body and vice versa. These two work together; neither side can be ignored.

Taking medicine is not wrong in principle; what is wrong is to attend only to the body and ignore the mind.

If there is a need for medicine, then take it, but be careful that you don't let it be a support and become dependent.

When the mind is kept free from tension and worry, sleep comes naturally. Or, even if you can't sleep, there will be such peace and calm that you will still feel refreshed.

Learn to be your own spiritual doctor. Whatever the nature of illness – heart problems, cancer or simply intense pain – it is through the power of meditation, the remembrance of God, that illness can be overcome. This will also protect you from the negative things your friends and even doctors might say about your health.

Sometimes even just hearing about another's illness makes people worry about getting it themselves. If there is something wrong with you, worrying about it and spreading your worry to others will only aggravate your ill-health.

So even if the body is sick, learn how to let the mind simply remain in the remembrance of God. If there is even a trace of worry, no cure can be effective.

WORRY

Worry and sorrow come from remembering past relationships, possessions, or problems in the home or at work. It's as if these things exert a relentless influence over you – imprisoning you.
Even if there has been a mistake, don't let the mind worry.

Worrying prevents you from filling yourself with love from God.
It is possible to fill the mind with so much love from God that there is no more room to add any worries.
Eliminating worries in this way restores the strength of happiness.

TRAPS

Keep yourself free from traps

Traps are:
thoughts about others
criticism of others
criticism of the self
doubt in the self...

Exaggerating a problem is also a trap.

You free yourself by:
creating only pure thoughts (about your eternal self and others);
cultivating good wishes for others (whatever their behaviour towards you);
maintaining God's remembrance (to be able to remain true).

If somebody comes and insults you especially in front of others (a trap!),
just think, 'This is a test' and you will be free.

Every thought which keeps you spiritual – unable to take something personally
– will liberate you from all traps.

REMOVING UNWORTHY HABITS

First of all, don't be afraid of your sins, because God will never stop loving you.

He knows that love keeps a child growing.
So just keep thinking of what He wants you to do – and do it

'Trying to do' will not work. 'Trying' does not bring a reward.
God's help comes only when there has been effort from the heart.

Having understood deeply what you want to see changed, sit with God and ask His forgiveness.
He always gives it, anyway.

Then share, ceaselessly, your experiences with others.
This is a spiritual charity which settles accounts, which is all that sin is, anyway.

Then you'll begin to feel cleaner, lighter and nearer to God, and the reminder to others that they can be, too.

TESTING YOUR SELF-RESPECT

Instead of waiting for someone to fill you with their respect, fill yourself with Godliness.
Let Godliness be visible in your life.
Godliness makes you worthy.

Don't be upset if you are shown disregard. Speak to a third party to check your behaviour.
If you haven't done anything wrong and your attitude is right, understand that the situation is a test of your ability to remain beyond the judgements of others.

Many such situations will come to test you.
Understand them as a test of your self-respect. They are a test of your self-love and patience.

Fill all the gaps in your own sense of self by continuing to explore your true spiritual worth.
As this awareness follows through into action, you will find it easy to respect others.

When you are full, it is easy to make others full.
When you are full, you pass all your tests.
And passing all tests makes you worthy of the respect of others.

PROTECTION

If I don't know the enemy,
I will be poorly equipped to protect myself.

Anger, greed, ego, lust, attachment are the enemies in myself and in others.
If I can't protect myself against them, who will?

Not to know the value of thoughts, or to move through life without an aim, is
ignorance.
This is another kind of enemy.
To say, 'Things are okay as they are', means that I have not yet recognised my
ignorance nor my need for protection.

The non-violent battle I have set out to win is of overcoming the vices.
Spirituality, playing itself out as virtue and wisdom in my life, is my sword and
my protection.

DESIRES

Desires are not the problem,
satisfying them is.

God says, 'Tell me all your desires and I will fulfil them', but people don't do this.
They turn to others expecting someone else to fulfil them.
Expectations are another kind of desire

Expecting to be praised, or recognised, or approved of are the signs of little
spiritual accomplishment.
Over time, this will deplete you.
Your work will turn superficial, for namesake only, and you will be distanced
from the true blessing of others.

God's pure desire is that we now become like Him.
Our only desire should now be that, too.

GRADES OF TOLERANCE

There are three grades of tolerance:
to endure a situation, with a lot of obvious effort,
to adapt, and to deal with a situation, using spiritual power to pass right through
it, not even noticing that something needs tolerating.

The sign of insufficient tolerance is:
the minute someone says any little thing you start complaining or crying.
It doesn't seem right to be so sensitive.
However, it isn't right to be insensitive either.

Understand with love what other people are saying.
Be sensitive to how others feel about what you say.

Some are amazed that others take what they say so badly. They say harsh things
to others, yet cannot tolerate being told anything themselves.

Lack of tolerance creates impatience, which diminishes the spirituality – the
quality of love – in the atmosphere.

'How long do I have to go on like this?'
This is not using tolerance as a power.
Remember, you are an actor on the stage of life.
Step back. Play your part with detachment.

Persevere in your spiritual efforts and simply pass to the next grade!

MISTAKES

Expand your awareness a little and mistakes no longer need to make you feel guilty.

For example, if you saw your life as an actor does his play, you would see one scene unfolding after another.

Each passing scene, having passed, is now over.
Wisdom says: 'This is how to see it.'

Letting bygones be bygones is easier if you remember that you cannot change the past, but you definitely can change the future.

You can change, here and now so that a mistake is not repeated.
Connection with God gives you so much power that your faults can be erased.

CHECKING THE SELF

No matter how good a car or its driver, if the car isn't regularly checked there will be problems.

In the same way, if one moment I am happy, but in the next moment I am not, something is wrong with the vehicle of my mind, and I will need to check it out.

Check the smoothness of its flow.
Is there purity? Has there been truth?
What about ego versus self-generated respect?
How much grief am I causing another?
Where are my weaknesses? How can I grow?

Checking these regularly and keeping them in shape will deliver you to the destination.

Carelessness in this will slow you down – like getting stuck in a storm.
You will feel yourself in a rut.

So, instead, keep yourself tuned and ever-ready.
Meditate at length, take power and love.
Teach yourself how to be generous-spirited and never stop giving.

CHANGING THOUGHTS

Thoughts are like seeds.
As are my thoughts, so will be my attitude and behaviour.
Therefore, my focus shouldn't be so much on wrong behaviour as on the thinking which causes it.

I need to be aware of how much damage is caused by negative thoughts.
Negative, wasteful thinking over a long period of time will put me right back into gutter.

The task of a student of spirituality is to change situations through thoughts.
I must change myself first, and then I can change the world.

PART 4

MOVING ONWARD – DISCOVERING TRUE LOVE

DADI'S FIRST THOUGHTS...

MODERN LOVE has come out of the heart and gone into the head. This is why we suffer headaches, because the head instead of heart has started to look for love. The poor heart has lost love and is unhappy. Whatever the age, young or even old – even small children – everybody is looking for love.

If we go inside ourselves, it is there we will discover what love is. If we look for it externally, we will need to keep on looking because we will find only deception and sorrow. We have to go inside to look for love.

People have lost faith in love. First there was the search to experience the unconditional love of God. When this was unsuccessful, faith in God was lost. As people then searched for love from each other, still without success, faith in love was lost.

There is a lot of misunderstanding about love. True love is not selfish love. The sign of selfish love is that a relationship will finish if we don't receive what we desire. Today there is selfishness within every kind of relationship – even within a relationship of mother and child or husband and wife. Selfish love always appears as one thing on the outside, but is completely different on the inside.

Deception like this has made the heart very unhappy. Whatever love was there has turned to hate. When we end up feeling threatened by a relationship, unsure of where it is going to take us, our love will turn to hate. Many believe they have found true love, only to discover later that they have been deceived. Because there is no more honesty in the heart, the heart is broken.

Deceptive love is love where there is no honesty in the heart. It creates dependency, and looks more like a deal than a relationship. This kind of love has become like a drug. We don't want love that is going to make us dependent. Love should be such that it makes honesty and truth, grow. It is honesty that shows us what love is, and real love shows us what honesty is.

The way to free ourselves from dependency on false love is to experience the fullness, the sweetness, of love that is true. Replace poison with nectar and it will be easy to recognise the worthlessness of false love. We should not just accept whatever love comes our way – from here, there, everywhere. If somebody wants to give us love, first see what kind of love they are offering. Our intuition should realise very quickly what kind of love it is.

To experience true love we should ask: 'Is my heart clean? Is it honest? Is it open?' If it isn't, if my heart is still broken, I will not be able to experience true love.

Some people don't want to have anything more to do with love. Because there has been deception from all sides, they have kicked love away. They think it is too complicated, too tiring. They say: 'I am not going to love anyone anymore and I don't want anyone to love me either.' They don't even want to talk about it. They don't want to hear about motherly love, friendly love, any kind of love at all.

These are the ones who end up saying, 'I just want to be alone.' They think that love should mean freedom from all these things. Actually, this is a kind of arrogance. Such people do not understand that this earth is a field of action, and that this field and our being on it, depends on the water of love.

Life without love is like life in a jungle. What is life like in the jungle? We are constantly afraid of what might come to us. We are isolated, not receiving any support from anywhere.

People don't know how to give love, nor do they know how to receive. Thus the heart is empty. This is why they don't know what love is. Actually, just to take the time and effort to understand what love is, is in itself an act of love.

True love is totally uninterested in that which is false. Superficial emotions which keep us on the surface of things are not the basis of true love. True love means pure love, and pure love is based on our innermost truth, goodness and desire to bring benefit to others. Being superficial and imagining things about others dilute pure love. Being affected by other people's character also dilutes it. We need to endeavour to understand the things of pure love and to check that this is what we are working with.

Let our love be so true that even if others become our enemy, we do not stop loving them. We have to give love truthfully, from our heart. Our love should be such that we are able to place our hand on our heart and know that what we are giving is true. True love is what everyone wants, so this is what we should share.

God gives us true love. The key to being able to fill ourselves with it is honesty. I have never hidden anything from God. I can't. He knows my heart very well and I know Him very well, too. The virtue of remaining honest with God enables the soul to receive so much from Him. When there is true love in our hearts for God, then in return we receive true love from God.

The results of pure, true love are always positive. Those with pure love are never influenced by anyone. Their ability to discern never diminishes. When our love is pure, others feel that our intentions are pure. There will be love in our vision. And there will be kindness in that love. In pure love there is always kindness.

I have always been very cautious not to separate myself from God's love, not to distance myself even in the slightest, thereby cutting myself off from the experience of His love. I am also careful that my intellect does not become engaged elsewhere, so that God can use it whenever He wants. This is why my heart is always happy and my head stays cool. I don't let just anything into my heart, which would then take me a lot of time and effort to remove.

When we start thinking about the past, present and future, old feelings will stir in our hearts, all at the same time, and it will take a lot of hard work to remove them. How will God be able to give us love; how will we be able to experience His love, if we are always so busy in that?

God's love actually changes me internally. Through God's love, everything old finishes. God's love makes me like a mirror – a mirror in which I can see myself clearly and through which others can see themselves – in no time at all.

The power of the love of God, the Almighty Authority, has accumulated in my soul. Because of God's love, my heart has become so strong that even if somebody does something to hurt me, I don't allow myself to get hurt. No matter what somebody might say, they cannot hurt me.

The experience of God's love restores faith in God. However, for this faith to be powerful, it needs to be based not just on feelings and experiences but also on a clear understanding of the true nature of the self, God, and life. This makes the soul worthy and powerful. God gives us such deep, powerful love that this love becomes eternal. It is never destroyed; it can never be reduced. Our love should remain eternal, too.

When I first came to London, people used to ask if I was married, and if I had any children. I would say: 'Yes, I have one Husband, who loves me very much and is very good to me. He has freed me from this world of deception by making me belong to Him. If there is anything in my heart, anything at all that hurts, His love is such that it just erases all the pain. This is why I call Him "Dilaram", the Comforter of Hearts. And yes, I have two children: Patience and Peace. So see, how full and happy my life has become.'

Patience and peace are like the mother and father of love. Where there is patience and peace, there can be a lot of give and take of love. Where there is no patience or peace, there can be no love. Patience and peace make us able to love others in a constant and steadfast way.

GOING BEYOND

The effort you need to be making now is to come close to God.
To experience this, practice going beyond the limited consciousness of yourself (body consciousness) until eventually you can remain in a state of constant, unlimited, spiritual awareness (soul-consciousness).

This is one of the most difficult things for any human being to achieve, because we have incarnated in many bodies and have had so many relationships.
Connection with God makes it possible to remain detached even while you are in the body and involved in human relationships.

In order to make such connection with God, you must cut off all other attachments.
Yet they must be cut with love.
Take help from God and learn how to cut them yourself.

GIVING YOUR HEART TO ONE

One task of those of us on a spiritual path is to help others experience belonging to God.
This means helping them identify with their spiritual personality.

I shall be able to do that only when I have effected this transformation myself.
The challenge in this comes in two varieties: the influence of those around me, and the more subtle influences from deep within my own self.
The former are easier to deal with, because their potential for causing me pain is usually clear and visible.
The latter (ego for example) take more time because they are subtle, and thus harder to recognise and face.

When I give my heart to God alone, there is nothing but joy.
Giving it to humans can create joy but also sorrow, because my original feelings of elevated, spiritual love for all are reduced to the limited.
The feeling of universal love is replaced by an attraction to only some.
This is not a basis for constant joy.

When I subject myself again and again to the limited emotions, my spiritual personality suffers.
It is a most subtle form of dishonesty, as I am not supposed to be an example of the limited but, rather, a model of the Divine.
My aim is not to make others like me, but to make them like God.

KNOWLEDGE

If I am a truly knowledgeable soul, I will be skilful in the things of the spirit.
I will be centred successfully in my spiritual identity.
I will be free from the influence of my past.
There will be only peace and happiness within.

True knowledge isn't a question of intellectual understanding alone.
It is for incorporating in my daily life, in order to improve it.
My every thought, word and action becomes naturally aligned with the laws of the universe. All that has ever gone wrong begins to be put right.

This 'knowing' protects me from small-minded ways of seeing and thinking of others.
It enables me to feel love for everyone but without the loss that occurs when you go too far into the matters of others.

This is the duty of those who have understood the self in depth.

Intellectual arrogance is the sign that I have not become truly knowledgeable.
True knowledge puts me in touch with the sweetness of life and makes me equally sweet.

ETHICS

Ethics is a code of conduct which promotes virtue and character.
There needs to be ethics in my personal, social and professional life.
To be ethical means to have a code of conduct for the self.

A personal code of conduct can be maintained when the intellect is not easily shaken by small matters.
For this reason, it is useful to have self-discipline. Self-discipline makes everything accurate, beautiful, spiritual and simple.

It is easy to have good relations with somebody who has good self-discipline.

The first level of ethics and code of conduct is to have a generous heart. When your heart is not generous, there is distress; you can neither do what you want nor communicate clearly. You cannot even co-operate with others. Feeling always low on energy, you will be cautious about how much you give.
A generous heart is not a question of giving money, but a state of relating to everyone as an equal.

INTEGRITY

Anybody who wants to be instrumental in serving the world needs to know how to work with integrity.

Integrity elevates character and brings internal power. It reveals a pure attitude. Those with integrity maintain great humility, even while holding positions of high status and commanding a lot of respect. They do not alter their character or virtues according to whom they are with.

They have pride in themselves.

Integrity over a long period of time makes the soul powerful. The intellect is clear and does not mix truth with falsehood.

A person with integrity is able to reveal truth through words spoken with wisdom. He or she never feels the need to prove truth.

Because a clear conscience is the reward of such honesty, a person with integrity considers the consequences of every action and is never drawn mindlessly into anything.

To behave in any lesser way is to deceive people.

CONTENTMENT

First of all, understand discontentment.
Discontent is caused by a constant multiplication of desires.
One desire leads to another until there's never a moment when you feel fulfilled.

Desires are like traps.
Because of endless desires, relationships have become very fragile.
There is a lot of irritability and anger due to:
selfish attachments (to possessions and people)
and pride (attachment to a particular image of the self).
Where there is discontentment, the heart can never be still because wasteful, negative thoughts destroy peace.

Contentment is the result of spiritual awareness, which allows you to recognise negativity.
It changes your pattern of thinking.
As you tap your huge inner potential, all desires are fulfilled and you regain your peace.

THOUGHT POWER

Through our thoughts, we are either gaining power or losing it.
With pure thoughts power is generated, and with impure thoughts power is destroyed.

Pure thoughts are those that express our spiritual personality.
Impure thoughts are all the others. They have nothing to do with our truth.
Thought is the vehicle which takes us from our non-spiritual self to our truth.

Spiritual knowledge is like a sieve through which we can filter out the untrue.
Running our thoughts through it constantly ensures that we are heading in the right direction.

When thoughts are brought into our action, they can be seen immediately.
When the mind is filled with virtues, they will be revealed in our actions.
By elevating our thoughts, we can literally end up purifying the self, inspiring others to do likewise. Our life will be the inspiration for them to change.
There won't even be the need to say anything.

Our vibrations of pure thought can reach out and touch the whole world.
Our very life can do the work of a lighthouse.

HAPPINESS

There is no nourishment like happiness
(it's an elixir).

There is no sickness like sorrow
(it's a poison).

Having been sorrowful for so long, the soul is now desperate for peace,
there can be no real happiness until the soul finds its peace.

Deep inner Peace, the kind born of union with God, gives so much power.
You forget about sorrow completely; there's only gratitude in the heart and so
much joy.
The experience of true happiness cures the sickness of sorrow.

This is a remedy not just to create happiness and joy in your life,
but to create it in the world also.
A cheerful face goes a long way towards making everything better!

CREATING PEACE

Peace will be created by coming face to face with the real things that are tearing our human family apart.

Greed, anger, ego attachment and lust have destroyed peace, so there is too much sorrow in the world.

It's not a question of going off to remote places of quiet or following a path that turns you away from the world.

It is a question of learning humility and emerging humanity's mercy.

Surrendering myself to God is the beginning.
Together, we can then create peace.

LOVE

If your companion is God, then even if you are alone, you will never feel lonely.

Happiness will be yours whether you are with other people or not.
God's love produces a variety of such magic.
It enables us to interact with love and co-operation.
It makes us into sources of mutual inspiration.
With worldly love, there is sometimes the concern that this is going to interfere with one's career or studies.
But love for God only enhances your ability to perform, on all levels.

TRUST

Trust is essential if you want to help people.
There are two aspects of trust – your own trust in others and their trust in you.
People will naturally start trusting you when they see you overcoming problems
in a reliable and constant way.
However, a more powerful and long-term way of gaining people's trust is to give
them the experience of your trust in them.

This is an art which can be cultivated as follows:
never listen to gossip and never foster it yourself;
form neither judgements nor opinions;
rather, be spiritual and clean in your feelings.
Learn to develop good wishes for others.
This will be the ultimate measure of your ability to trust.

TRUE RESPECT

People like to be shown respect; many believe it to be a right.
However, as in the case of most rights, there is a responsibility attached to it. This responsibility needs to be understood in order for us to become worthy of respect.

True respect does not come from what we do, as much as how well we do it. This means that we are shown respect according to the virtues and qualities revealed through our behaviour.

Respect is not a matter of supply and demand.
On the contrary, if people pick up that we are even slightly in need of respect, they will usually turn away from us completely.

This is because the need to be respected indicates a gap somewhere in our sense of self – and most people are so busy trying to fill their own gaps, they get annoyed at the prospect of having to fill someone else's.

Be suspicious of any desire on your part for respect. Indeed, such thoughts are a sure sign that no one is going to give it to you anyway.
The very act of trying to get respect from others proves you to be unworthy of it.

SPIRITUAL EDUCATION

A spiritual education teaches how to keep the mind free from tension and fluctuations.
An unsteady mind is the result of letting yourself be strongly influenced by human situations.
Spiritual awareness keeps you centred and thus protected.
You claim increasing happiness and help others to do the same.

The world is a supermarket of sorrow. Don't buy any!
A good spiritual education teaches you how to be discerning in your shopping.

Refuse to accept anything but happiness from others, as well as the world.

BEING A TEACHER

Teaching others is best done with subtlety, explaining in such a way that the mind opens because the heart has understood.

Aim to inspire, rather than teach.
My love for those I teach will do that.
My love for God will do that.
To the extent that I am soul-conscious when teaching, so others will have this experience.

Never force anyone to make spiritual effort.
When the mind opens, this happens naturally.
Avoid making comparisons. It creates loss of hope.
Harbour no ill will and never try to score a point.

Be like the parent whose love for the child is what makes him grow.

SPIRTUAL PROGRESS

There is benefit for you in every situation. That is, if, you know how to look for it.

The idea behind steady spiritual progress is to see every circumstance and situation (particularly those that challenge you) as a tailor-made lesson in your personal plan for self-development.

For example, in a situation where hurtful or angry words were exchanged, why not see it as the chance either to perceive things about your own character which need changing, or to rehearse some virtue or quality that you need to put into practice more often?
Actually, we should be grateful for the opportunity to evaluate ourselves.

In this way you can transform anything into a constructive lesson.
Never think that you've learned enough and now can stop.
You should love it when people try to correct you or give you advice. It keeps you alert and gives you plenty of opportunity to put your truth into practice.
It's a sign of great danger to be unable to accept criticism and instead use your understanding to criticise others.
Realise deeply the significance of every moment, and your spiritual progress will be assured.

PART 5

JOURNEY'S END – KNOWING GOD

DADI'S FIRST THOUGHTS...

⌒⌒

ONE OF the first experiences I had on coming to the Brahma Kumaris organisation at its inception in the late 1930s, was of feeling myself linked to God as if by a current of electricity. There was just this stream of electricity flowing directly from God to me. It was such an exhilarating experience that I knew that all I wanted to do was turn myself and my life over to God completely. Later, I began to feel as if God Himself had taken hold of my hand, and that it was He who was making me move forward. I still feel that way today. I feel His company constantly and the hand of His blessings always on my head.

My experience is that you cannot see God with these physical eyes and you cannot understand God with a limited, gross intellect. Rather, God needs to be recognised, which is something far more revelatory than mere 'seeing' or philosophical understanding. 'Recognition' is not the domain of the physical brain as much as it is one of the heart. When the *heart* sees God, when the *heart* knows God, then there can be recognition. Thus, recognition is a result of feelings, experiences and understandings that come from the heart.

The first thing to recognise and understand is that God is One. He is unique; there can be no one but the one God alone who is called God. We need to understand that human beings are only human; that with humans there can be upheavals. The gods and the goddesses of mythology and the idols and deities of the East were elevated beings, worthy of being worshipped, but who made them so elevated? It was God.

Understanding these things helped me to recognise God. Before coming to this organisation, I believed in God in a devotional way. This means that although I had faith, there were no real, tangible experiences of who God was. Now my heart says: 'I have seen God; I know God.' I have recognised God from the heart.

Human beings believe that in order to understand something, you have to think about it. However, to understand God you don't have to think. When it comes to physical matters, then there is a need for thinking – you need to analyse in order to figure it out. But not with God. Haven't you ever had a thought simply come to you 'out of the blue' – an intuition, or a sudden inspiration – without any actual thinking? God gave you that inspiration. Did you do any thinking? In one flash, God gave you that understanding. You didn't think, but suddenly the whole thing was clear to you, whereas under ordinary circumstances you wouldn't have got the picture even if you had thought about it for years. God gave you that intuition. He touched your intellect, your heart, like light.

It is truly a wondrous thing that God can touch us in this way, while He Himself is beyond thoughts. God does not think. God doesn't have the need to create any thoughts. And now He is making us like Himself – beyond wasteful and ordinary thoughts, beyond thought altogether. Actually, there is no need to think. Thinking too much is just a habit.

God does so much, yet He is beyond the feeling of doing. He does not think, yet still you say that He thinks. That is His wonderful personality. We cannot become God, because His part is unique. But as His children, we can become like Him. And this is all that God wants us to do.

God is very happy to see us making the effort to become like Him. When we are not making this effort, He does not like it at all. This is because He is not just our Mother and Father, but He is our Teacher as well. A teacher is never happy when the students do not study well. God has given us understanding, made us belong to Him and is sustaining us in such a way that we are becoming like Him. Of course, there is a great difference between the Supreme soul and other souls, but still it is not difficult to become like Him. The more we can become like God and serve, the more we can become truly accurate instruments for His task. Then we can enjoy His Company even more. God wants us to become like Him, and we want to become like God, so the desire of both parties is being fulfilled.

To become like the Father means that whatever the qualities, virtues and powers God has, He gives them to us. They are given in the form of an inheritance. He feels that we are worthy and therefore He gives then as His inheritance. The virtues and the powers that God gives us make it easy for us to become like Him. When we become like Him, then whatever He wants to do, He is able to do through us. So why should we not claim our inheritance from God? After all, He is not only God. He is our Father, too.

This is the corporeal world where the sun rises and sets, day turns into night and night into day, and the tides go in and out. It is a world of constant motion. However, in the Soul World, where God resides, all is eternal, constant, stable and stationary. There are no changes whatsoever. It is beyond this world of five elements. It is an experience of complete stillness.

We leave the Soul World and take birth in the physical body, which is made of matter. The result is that we experience duality in life – changes and contrasts such as sorrow and happiness and so on. But God does not come into the cycle of birth and death, and so in the Soul World there is only stillness. As we learn to go to that Home and be with God, we too become constant and still.

We leave our original Home (the Soul World), come into the drama of life and eventually we forget the plot. God never comes into the drama, and therefore does not ever forget the plot. Thus, it is He alone who can give us the understanding of the whole play. Only God possesses such knowledge; only He can come and give it. This is why He is the Supreme Soul. He is beyond, He is different; He is unique. He is the Father, and He gives us new life.

God is wonderful, you know. Even though He is not in the drama, He has the complete knowledge of the drama. He does not have to experience it to know it. He does not have eyes, but He sees our experiences. And He gives us recognition so that we can 'see' and know Him. Just as generator sits in one place, continuously sending out an electric current, so the Almighty Father keeps sending us spiritual power. And we receive it – if, that is, we are linked properly and have taken care that no part has blown its fuse.

God is the Director of the drama on this world stage, so He knows everything that's going on in the drama. In spite of this, it is not that He would give the whole plot away. He tells us only that which is necessary to know. As the Director, God helps us to understand this drama as it is, and to act accordingly. The drama moves along very slowly, so we should not hurry or worry. See the drama, understand it, and play our role. This is the training God gives us.

Previously we used to complain, 'Oh God, you are not listening to me; you are not helping me; you are not coming to me.' Although it is true that God is the Director, He also has to act out His part according to the plot. This means that God cannot come even a second before His time in the drama.

God's role at this time in the drama is to enable us to have a relationship with Him. Being in His Company in this way, I can be of help to God and thereby create my fortune. We start feeling the concern to play a good role in the drama and to play it well, without laziness.

Attraction to bodily names and forms has taken us away from God. This in turn has made us search for God, just as when someone has lost his beloved and he longs to be with her again. Another example is a lost child. A lost child, discovered by a stranger, will never find comfort, no matter what is offered as a consolation. The child will just continue to cry and cry. Why? Because he wants his mother. So why do we cry? We may have a good home, good parents, a good family, but still we cry because it is the soul that is lost, and all it wants is the eternal Mother, the eternal Father.

Once we find God, we stop crying. The search ends. It is just like the moment that the lost child is finally reunited with his mother – anything he has been given to distract himself is just discarded – and he runs to her in such relief.

The plight of a seeker is understandable. It is the same as the plight of someone who is lost. 'Oh God, where are You? Do you really exist? When will that day come when I will meet You?' There are many such seekers whose thirst has not yet been quenched. Their desire still remains. This desperate state remains until God is recognised.

As our understanding and recognition of God grows, so does our love. Yoga becomes an intense experience of being absorbed in that love. The effect is like that of fire – everything is transformed. In this 'fire of yoga' you are entirely consumed by the sweetness of God's remembrance and the experience of all relationships with Him. We are made so clear and refined that there is the literal experience of becoming angelic. This is the power of God's love for us. If God didn't love us, we would never be able to achieve such heights.

I feel that God is doing so much for me personally. It is God's love which is purifying me and filling me with spiritual might and mastery. It is His love which has filled me with quietness and tranquillity. Because He is always with me, I never feel alone. He is making us into angels, the true companions of God.

SPIRITUALITY

Spirituality is the art of balancing your responsibilities:
to yourself, to your family and to the world.
The basis for this is a deep understanding of the self, God and the law of cause and effect (karma).

Knowing the self enables you to be detached from physical factors and their limitations.
Knowing God enables you to create a deep link of love and draw into yourself all attributes, virtues and powers from the Source.
Understanding the deep philosophy of karma motivates you to settle debts of the past and perform elevated action now.

Anyone can fall victim to the suffering of a poor state of mind, ill-health, loss of wealth or unhappy relationships.
Human life depends on these four factors and yet each of them has become so fragile and unreliable.
God's power restores tolerance and the ability to face anything.
An understanding of the deep philosophy of karma reveals how elevated thoughts, pure feelings and good actions can resolve all difficulties for the self and for the world.

GOD THE ALMIGHTY

Why is God known as the 'Almighty'?
It is because He has 'All Might' which He then offers to us children in the form of an inheritance.

He draws us to Him, filling us with power, so that we can experience all aspects of truth.

Through God's power our minds become clean and refreshed.
It is His power which takes us beyond the limited into the experiences of the Divine.

When we look at ourselves and at the world, every step of positive change is evidence of this Godly donation.

My connection with God is revealed through my character, relationships and my general outlook on life.

When I am feeling alone or weak, it means I am not letting God's power work for me.
Being incapable of co-operation or loveful feelings also implies that I am not experiencing the love of God.

Why should I not begin to claim my inheritance now?

GOD'S LIGHT

Many religions believe that God is Light.
The wisdom of God is also Light.
And those who study it become light and easy!

Who makes this Light?
God, from His own state of eternal enlightenment.
God, the Being of Light, makes the world around Him light, chasing away the
darkness of ignorance.
Light spreads from God, through His studious children, into the whole world.
Others receive this Light when they see the practical proof of it in the lives of
His effort-making children.

God gives His Light from above for this service.
The ones who catch it and share it will be happy, no matter how little may be
received in return from humans.

MERCY

God is known as the Ocean of Forgiveness and an experience of His mercy makes you feel that you have made a best friend for life.
Peace makes its home in your heart.

When you accept God's mercy for you, your perspective on life changes.
It is God's merciful vision that allows you to see your potential for perfection.
Then it becomes your turn to be merciful to yourself.
Mercy for the self means striving to be true to that image of perfection.

By drawing from God whatever power is needed, we can become whatever we wish.

GOD AS MY EVERYTHING

Do you realise the importance of having a relationship with God?

Having had numerous relationships with human beings over a long period of time, the soul has now become so depleted and tired that it is hardly able to remember its purpose, let alone achieve it.

Making God your friend will bring Him close, but in fact it is important not to limit your experience of God to just one kind of relationship.
Experience them all –
God as your Mother, Father, Companion, Beloved, Teacher, Guru, Child.
Each relationship brings so much sweetness.

If any one of these is lacking, you will be forced to take that support from a human being.
This is a mistake, because no human being at this time can offer you such consistent and unconditional love.
Don't content yourself with a mere intellectual understanding of these relationships.
Go into their depths and open yourself to the tangible experience of each.

BLESSINGS FROM GOD

When you understand that you belong to God, then God is responsible for you.
You are in His care

As love for God increases, spiritual understanding wells up inside you
and there is so much power that you feel, 'There is nothing I cannot accomplish'.

As God sees your love and faith, He gives more love and faith in return, and you
feel, 'My life is in His hands'.

To receive God's blessings, simply remember all that He is giving.
Keep it alive in your heart and be accountable.

God's blessings go only to those who are honest.

CONNECTION WITH GOD

The connection with God is automatic for those who have faith.

By faith I mean faith in life, as in the expression,
'Whatever has happened is good,
whatever is going to happen will be even better.'

To develop faith, let go of your arrogance and make your intellect clean.
Don't let yourself be influenced by anyone.

Listen to God with the consciousness of being His child.
Don't listen carelessly, listen attentively, with love and self-surrender.
Then, when thinking or simply talking to yourself, keep in mind what God has said.

The deeper your connection with God, the more power you receive.
Fear finishes.
Everything in your life begins to feel easy.
You become clean, sensible and good.

KNOWING GOD

How do you know when you have recognised God as He really is?

The main sign is you start to become like Him.

You take everything from its intrinsic, spiritual perspective; you see and interact
with everyone on the basis of your spiritual identity and theirs;
you are imperturbable, with a sense of values that is never undermined.

True recognition of God – who He is and what He gives –
makes you feel as if you belong to Him and He to you.
All He has becomes yours.

GOD AS DIRECTOR

The only thing we need to do is remember,
'I am a soul and around me is the Game of Life playing itself out'.

Then, whatever role comes up for me to play I'll play it very well, no longer confusing
the actor with the act.

The one who remembers this is, in God's eyes, a hero.
God says, 'Understand the part I have given you to play'.

But though I do not see myself as God sees me, I should never ask, 'How'?

God is the director and He understands me very well.
Realise this clearly: God understands you very well.

HELPING GOD

The best way to ensure that we are a help to God is to make sure we ourselves have taken maximum help from God.

He is not helped by our turning and asking Him to please give help to a particular someone.
God knows who needs help.
He'll give it without asking!

We help best by taking God's love and sharing it with others and finishing our own complaints.
There's danger in seeing the weakness of others. The mind tends to focus exclusively on that, just tiring itself out, being of benefit to no one.

Spiritual love makes the mind work right.
We want to help others see only the truth.
Good wishes and love are always the first step to the solution.
Loving our brothers and sisters is the solution.

DEVOTION AND WISDOM

Devotional feelings are pure ones consisting of sweetness and innocence.
They are feelings of faith in God, but they can be shaken.

Faith, without some wisdom to back it up, may fail you in a moment of need.

Both are needed for long-term spiritual attainment:
like feeling close to God and close to others, too, in an unshakable way.
Or having true feelings, no matter what, and becoming spiritually accomplished.

If either faith of wisdom is lacking, your life cannot function right.
It's like understanding your doctor's prescription, but somehow not trusting it anyway.
It leaves you feeling unsure.

So have a dialogue between your feelings and your understanding.
They need to know each other, and work together well!

THE INTELLECT

The intellect is the vessel which holds the knowledge of God.
It is different from the mind.

A clean intellect is like the mind's filter, sorting out thoughts of value from those of waste,
enabling me to put into action only that which is of value.
So much energy is saved in this way, enabling me to do more, better and in less time.

In India, in the olden days, each household kept a special vessel for water.
The first thing done in the early morning hours of every day was to empty the vessel and put in fresh water.

As the spiritual child of God, the least I can do is to clean the vessel of my intellect in the early morning hours of every day and fill it with spiritual truths.

Only when my intellect is clean and full will I then have something of value to offer others.

ETERNAL HAPPINESS

Eternal happiness comes when the mind and the senses have become quiet and peaceful. In that state, there is spiritual power; we are performing actions, but free from
desires and free from attachment to what we do.
Such happiness finishes any sorrow that may come to us. For example, if anybody comes to me now with unhappiness, I am able to remove it so that the whole atmosphere around me becomes one of great peace. Yes, of course, this has taken time, but it has definitely happened.

Eternal happiness means the happiness that stays with you.forever, so that even if it feels as if it is running out, you only need to evoke the memory of it.
Before I began these studies, I had reached a point in my life where happiness had disappeared, and I was filled with the desire to experience it.
And now, today, that is where I am drawn again and again; into that experience of eternal happiness.

NEWNESS

It is possible to become happy, free, and deeply peaceful and bring into your life the literal, tangible companionship of God.

These are extraordinary times for reaching towards your highest ideals.

WALKING THE SPIRITUAL PATH

We who walk the spiritual path are those who have enrolled ourselves in the school of spirituality.

Our aim should be to pass all subjects, with honour.

This means that spiritual understanding and power from God have been so assimilated that not one of life's many challenges is faced without equanimity and truth.

The heart is merciful and altruistic, never giving or taking sorrow.

Feelings are pure, that is, devoid of any needs or expectations, and these pure feelings are shared abundantly with others.

And we'll not have achieved this by becoming a hermit and leaving the world of everyday life; rather, we'll have remained completely in the world, yet distanced from all its vice and negativity.

Now is the time to become such a successful student of life;

I should never doubt myself in this.

Trust in God incurs His assistance.

This plus my own determination will create strength to move forward and progress.

God is giving me everything.

Have faith in this and proceed comfortably on the path to becoming like Him.

ALPHBETICAL LIST OF THEMES

BRAHMA KUMARIS CENTRES

WORLD HEADQUARTERS
PO Box No 2, Mount Abu 307501, RAJASTHAN, INDIA
Tel: (+91) 2974 - 238261 to 68 Fax: (+91) 2974 - 238883
E-mail: abu@bkivv.org

INTERNATIONAL CO-ORDINATING OFFICE
& REGIONAL OFFICE FOR EUROPE AND THE MIDDLE EAST
Global Co-operation House, 65-69 Pound Lane, London, NW10 2HH, UK
Tel: (+44) 208 727 3350 Fax: (+44) 208 727 3351
E-mail: london@bkwsu.org

AFRICA
Global Museum for a Better World, Maua Close, off Parklands Road, Westlands
PO Box 123, Sarit Centre, Nairobi, Kenya
Tel: (+254) 20-374 3572 Fax: (+254) 20-374 3885
E-mail: nairobi@bkwsu.org

AUSTRALIA AND SOUTH EAST ASIA
78 Alt Street, Ashfield, Sydney, NSW 2131, Australia
Tel: (+61) 2 9716 7066 Fax: (+61) 2 9716 7795
E-mail: ashfield@au.bkwsu.org

THE AMERICAS AND THE CARIBBEAN
Global Harmony House, 46 S. Middle Neck Road, Great Neck, NY 11021, USA
Tel: (+1) 516 773 0971 Fax: (+1) 516 773 0976
E-mail: newyork@bkwsu.org

RUSSIA, CIS AND THE BALTIC COUNTRIES
2 Gospitalnaya Ploschad, build. 1, Moscow - 111020, Russia
Tel: (+7) 495 263 02 47 Fax: (+7) 495 261 32 24
E-mail: moscow@bkwsu.org

www.bkpublications.com
E-mail: enquiries@bkpublications.com

OTHER BOOKS TO FEED THE SOUL

If you have enjoyed this book, you might like the following to enhance your meditation practice and deepen your spiritual understanding. The insights and personal experiences expressed within these works have been derived from the knowledge and practice of the ancient practice of Raja Yoga Meditation. We Brahma Kumaris Publications hope that you too will find amongst these jewels of wisdom, a new perspective and awareness for living to achieve the inner serenity that many have found.

Wings of Soul
Dadi Janki

Dadi Janki is a yogi – one who seeks union with God. Her life's work has been to build within herself the experience of the Divine and to share that experience with the world. This book gives deep insights into the true original nature of the self, God, spirituality in daily life and world peace.

Order Code: 2104, Price: £7.00
2nd Edition 1999, ISBN 978-1-558746725
140mm x 214mm, 137 Pages, Paperback

The Gift of Peace
Brahma Kumaris

Distilled from the rich fruits of spiritual study, simple and true thoughts are shared for practical use. Dip into this collection daily and experience the peace and power when applying these thoughts in your life. Essential reading for anyone yearning to experience peace within.

Order Code: 2150, Price: £2.50
2nd Edition 2009, ISBN 978-1-886872240
105mm x 148mm, 98 Pages, Paperback

Practical Meditation
BK Jayanti

An accessible guide to Raja Yoga meditation by a dynamic and highly regarded spiritual leader. Worldrenowned spiritual leader and yogi Sister Jayanti guides you through the simple yet effective steps to beginning a transformational meditation program using the Raja Yoga technique.

Order Code: 2015, Price: £10.00
1st Edition 2008, ISBN 1-4027-6626-2
145mm x 165mm, 112 Pages, Hardback

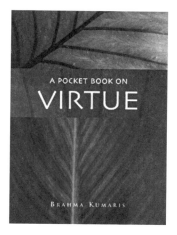

A Pocket Book on Virtue
Dadi Janki

This little book contains a surprisingly rich blend of affirmations and inspirations about bringing virtue back into life. Practical methods and suggestions for dealing with real-life situations sit side-by-side with timeless thoughts on the soul's journey to perfection. Being virtuous is not about an austere religious experience away from the reality of day-to-day life, it's simply about being who we are and doing what we want to do, but being it and doing it better.

Order Code: 2132, Price: £2.50
3rd Edition 2006, ISBN 978-1-886872233
105mm x 147mm, 80 Pages, Paperback

Food & Soul Vegetarian Cookbook
Brahma Kumaris

Easy and tasty vegetarian recipes appear in this book, with rich colour photographs and simple instructions for a variety of delights, including appetisers, soups, main dishes, sauces, desserts, cakes, breads, pastries, drinks, jams etc.

Order Code: 2132, Price: £2.50
3rd Edition 2006, ISBN 978-1-886872233
105mm x 147mm, 80 Pages, Paperback

Pure & Simple
Isik Polatar & Manju Patel

The secret of these mouthwatering dishes is that the recommended ingredients are fresh and pure, prepared in a way that maximises their natural goodness.

Pure & Simple contains:

- 108 deliciously different recipes
- dishes made from super-healthy vegetarian ingredients
- swift and simple instructions that are easy to follow
- inspirational thoughts to accompany each recipe
- usage of pure ingredients
- the results are simply delicious!

Order Code: 2205, Price: £12.50
2nd Edition 2009, ISBN 978-1-886872509
270mm x 240mm, 256 Pages, Paperback

Wisdom For The Day
Desk Calendar

A well-nourished heart is automatically giving and full of grace. We can nourish our hearts with the energy of positive thoughts and pure feelings. When we realise we are eternal souls, beings of consciousness rather than matter, and that our original nature is benevolent and wise, the heart grows full. When we remember, with love, that we are the offspring of an eternal Parent, a source of eternal truth, the heart overflows. This is the greatest gift we can offer to each other and the world in the year ahead.

Order Code: 3218, £8.81
148mm X 148mm, 368 pages

A variety of meditation commentaries, talks and music are available from
www.bkpublications.com